Gateway To Hope

For the Grieving Heart

REGINA CONLEY HOCKETT

DEDICATION

Life is a gift from God. Our children, family, friends, neighbors, and strangers are all gifts to be savored. Although some days may be full of hardship and sadness, each breath, heartbeat, and thought illustrates the beautiful gift of life. Keep the positive memories alive and thank God for the blessings in your past, present, and future. I dedicated this book to all Moms that has lost their children to violent murder. I pray that the words that are penned here will help you turn your mourning into joy. The best way OUT is always Through.

This book is for you and others that might have encountered in life a tragedy and are experiencing grief in the loss of a loved one to an act of violence.

This is what life presented to me as a challenge as a single mother with two children to raise, in a world that doesn't often display forgiveness, but retaliation and hatred. It was when I thought life was good, as I had good employment, owned my own home, my children were doing well, and personal relationships were blooming when the fatal choice to pull the trigger shattered this pictorial view – ending the life if my 12 year old daughter Adriane. The challenge to model love and forgiveness assisted me in healing the wound punctured deeply in my emotions, and to mentor other families of murder victims.
My mentorship crossed racial and denominational barriers as I transitioned into a greater life of victory.

Grief is a personal and highly individualized experience. How you grieve depends on many factors, including your personality and coping style, your life experience, your faith, and the nature of the loss. The grieving process takes time. Healing happens gradually; it can't be forced or hurried—and there is no "normal" timetable for grieving. Some people start to feel better in weeks or months. For others, the grieving process is measured in years. Whatever your grief experience, it's important to be patient with yourself and allow the process to naturally unfold.

There are 5 stages of Grief:

Denial: "This can't be happening to me."

Anger: "*Why* is this happening? Who is to blame?"

Bargaining: "Make this not happen, and in return I will _____."

Depression: "I'm too sad to do anything."

Acceptance: "I'm at peace with what happened."

If you are experiencing any of these emotions following a loss, it may help to know that your reaction is natural and that you'll heal in time. However, not everyone who grieves goes through all of these stages—and that's okay. When you're grieving, it's most important that you take care of yourself. The stress of a major loss can quickly deplete your energy and emotional reserve, being aware and addressing your physical and emotional needs will help you get through this difficult time. Don't let anyone tell you how to feel and plan ahead for triggers such as, anniversaries, holidays, birthdays and milestones.

The sadness of losing someone you love never goes away completely, but it shouldn't be your main focus. If the pain of the loss is so constant and severe that it keeps you from resuming your life, you may be suffering from a condition known as complicated grief. Complicated grief is like being stuck in a high state of mourning. You may have trouble accepting the death long after it has happened or be so preoccupied with the person who died that it disrupts your daily routine and undermines your other relationships.

Normal grief does not require the use of antidepressants. While medication may relieve some of the symptoms of grief, it cannot treat the cause, which is the loss itself. Furthermore, by numbing the pain that must be worked through, eventually, antidepressants delay the mourning process. Seek professional help if you need to. We sometimes think as Christians that we don't need it because we have God. God gifted these people to do what they do. Trust that He will also give them insight of what you are dealing with.

PRAYER: Lord, in all your awesome power, please be with me and direct every aspects of my being through this journey called grief. Give me wisdom in all decisions that I make that the instructions are from you. In Jesus Name, Amen

Parents' Grief

Many parents have to suffer the death of a child, at birth or at a very young age. There probably is no greater suffering than losing a child, since it so radically interferes with the desire of a father and mother to see their child grow up to be a beautiful, healthy, mature, and loving person. The great danger is that the death of a child can sometimes take away the parents' desire to live. It requires an enormous act of faith on the part of parents to truly believe that their children, however brief their lives, were given to them as a gift from God, to deepen and enrich their own lives.

Whenever parents can make that leap of faith, their children's short lives can become fruitful far beyond their expectations.

Regret of the past and dread of the future are both "thieves of joy." Begin right now to say, "I've got a future, and there's hope for me. God is on my side. No matter how many disappointments I have had in the past, this is a new day. Goodness and mercy are following me today." "Surely goodness and mercy shall follow me all the days of my life: and I will dwell in the house of the Lord forever." Psalm 23:6 If I am not experiencing joy in my life, I have allowed the thief to come in and steal it. I need to take it back by the words that come out of my mouth. Accept that your loss will offer you a new understanding. Trust God with all of your thoughts and feelings, even the negative ones. If you are struggling in your faith, cry out to Him. God is big enough to handle your expression of grief and sorrow. Accept God's leadership and live in the palm of His hand. Accept His peace and comfort and be obedient to His will. "…and provide for those who grieve in Zion—to bestow on them a crown of beauty instead of ashes, the oil of joy instead of mourning, and a garment of praise instead of a spirit of despair. They will be called oaks of righteousness, a planting of the Lord for the display of his splendor."

— Isaiah 61:3

"Those who cleanse themselves from the latter will be instruments for special purposes, made holy, useful to the Master and prepared to do any good work."

— 2 Timothy 2:21

PRAYER:
"Lord, thank You that I have hope and a future...because You are on my side." Thank you for loving me, even when I'm not so lovely. I am not just a speck on earth...You see and care about me. Just imagine my heavenly Father never takes His eyes off of me! Lord, thank you for loving me and letting me know that I am special to you. I know that you already have my life already worked out. You know my end and my beginning. Thank you for gathering my tears and showering them with your love when they flood my pillow in the darkness.

The Lord looks down from heaven and see's every person. From His throne He watches all who live on earth. He made their hearts and understands everything they do". Ps. 13:15 Is God concerned about me? God has a special plan for your life. God's gifts for you are the best gifts for you to possess. He has fashioned you in His image and tenderly knit you in your mother's womb. You are purposed to be a God-loving YOU.

The Lord said, "I have indeed seen the misery of my people in Egypt. I have heard them crying out because of their slave drivers, and I am concerned about their suffering. Just as in (Exodus 3:7 NIV) He is also concerned about you.

Moses was on the far side of the wilderness when God spoke to him through the burning bush. He had failed in Egypt and bailed to Midian. Yep, failed and bailed. He ran away to the wilderness where he stayed for the next forty years. Sometimes it is only on the far side of the wilderness that God can get our attention. Sometimes it is when we feel alone, abandoned, and forgotten that our ears are pricked to hear. Isolation is often God's place of invitation.

Now that you know the backstory, let's join Moses at his wakeup call. Now Moses was tending the flock of Jethro his father-in-law, the priest of Midian, and he led the flock to the far side of the wilderness and came to Horeb, the mountain of God. There the angel of the Lord appeared to him in flames of fire from within a bush. Moses saw that though the bush was on fire it did not burn up. So Moses thought, "I will go over and see this strange sight—why the bush does not burn up. "When the Lord saw that he had gone over to look, God called to him from within the bush, "Moses! Moses! "And Moses said, "Here I am" (Exod. 3:1–4).

Here's something interesting about this encounter. When God spoke, He didn't speak through a fragrant rose bush, God spoke through a prickly, thorny, dried up old desert shrub. Oh yes, when God chooses to speak through something or someone, any old bush will do. I don't know about you, but that gives me great hope! "When the Lord saw that he had gone over to look." When God saw that He had Moses' attention, He began to speak. I wonder how many times we have missed God's gentle whisper and tender tug because we not were paying attention. How many times has God tried to speak to us, but we were too busy to notice? Moses turned aside. God spoke.

"Do not come any closer," God said. "Take off your sandals, for the place where you are standing is holy ground." Then he said, "I am the God of your father, the God of Abraham, the God of Isaac and the God of Jacob." At this, Moses hid his face, because he was afraid to look at God. The Lord said, "I have indeed *seen* the misery of my people in Egypt. I have *heard* them crying out because of their slave drivers, and I am *concerned* about their suffering. So I have come down to *rescue* them from the hand of the Egyptians and to bring them up out of that land into a good and spacious land. God sees! This sounds really good to me!! How about you??

God hears!

God is concerned!

God will rescue!

No matter what you're going through today. Even if you HAVE failed and bailed, even if you are somewhere on the backside of the wilderness, God sees you. God hears you. God is concerned. And God will rescue. Perhaps He is waiting for you to turn aside to see the burning ashes in your own backyard. Make no mistake about it. He has not left you. Never has. Never will. He speaks to us and waits for us to turn aside and listen.

PRAYER: Lord, You are a good Father. You never change, grow weary of me, or tire of helping me. Your Word says you care, then I choose to trust in that care. I place every burden I carry in your hands today. Thank you for your loving care for me and all that is important to me. Teach me to trust you more and more every day. You care for me! I can, therefore, live a carefree life, free from heaviness, oblivious to the confusion and quandaries the enemy of my soul tries to engage me in. I hold on to Ps. 138:8. In Jesus' Name Amen

God's Plan

Everyone faces problems in their life. We all have disappointments, shattered dreams, people who don't like us, and people who even come against us. And the devil wants to use these things to discourage us and keep us from moving forward with our lives and the plans God has for us. He's a dream thief, and if he can get you to focus on what's wrong or what you don't like about your life, he can defeat you. When the Lord placed upon my heart to start the grass roots support group for mothers whose had children's lives were taken by violent murder, I felt that no one that has been through this would allow me to be a part of their lives to help through the grieving process. At the time, this was a really important issue to me, to be able to do this because of feeling like I went through this alone, except for the Holy Spirit. One day, I got a call from a mother that I reached out to after hearing about her son. She was a little hesitate to speak to me until after I shared my story. We connected immediately because we shared the same testimony concerning our children.

I received calls from several other moms that I reached out to that wanted to help me with reaching other moms. God has made a lot of things possible for Victorious Mothers of Murder, including opportunities to reach mothers in other cities. Until we agree with God, He cannot do anything in our lives. We have to learn to recognize the lies of Satan and stop believing him. We need to glance at our problems and stare at Jesus. Then we can have the mind of Christ and think like God thinks...

God has a plan for your life and the devil knows it. He will try to use fear to keep you in bondage and stop you from living the plan. When you fear, don't run!! The only way you can get to the other side of it is to dip both heels in, set you face like flint and say, "I know I've heard from God, and I am going forward. There is no fear in faith, SO FEAR, get out of the way. I'm moving forward!!!
Joshua (NKJ) 1:9 Have I nor commanded you? Be strong and vigorous, and very courageous. Be not afraid, neither be dismayed, for the Lord your God is with you wherever you go.

PRAYER: Lord, I ask for Your wisdom regarding my future, knowing that You give to everyone liberally and without reproach. I ask in faith, without doubting, expecting You to give me divine direction in every area of my life. I thank You in advance for the wisdom You assure me You will give. Help me to be strong and of good courage as you lead me in the way that I should go. Father, give me the courage to follow the pathway of faith, not the path of fear, for you have not given me a spirit of fear, but of power, love and a sound mind. Amen

Pray Without Ceasing:

Have you ever played tether ball as a child? It is a game that consist of a pole and a ball that hangs from a rope. You have two player that would have a turn to make the ball go to the right and one to the left. You have to be consistent in getting the ball to go to the side that you were chose to make it go. I want to stay connected to God like a tetherball is connected to the poll. Don't you? Whether the ball is moving or still, it is connected to the poll, securely tethered by a rope. Or whether you are moving or still can be connected to God, securely tethered by grace and strengthened in prayer.

The 18th chapter of Luke begins with Jesus telling his disciples a parable about a persistent widow. He told them this story to encourage them to pray continually and to not give up. (Luke 18:1 KJV) The widow, Jesus told them, wanted justice so she went to the judge and asked for favor against her adversary. The judge didn't care much about God or justice so he brushed her off and sent her away. But she kept going back and asking for justice, so finally the judge gave in because he didn't want her to bother him anymore.

Then Jesus explained the significance of the story to his friends:

"And the Lord said, "Listen to what the unjust judge says. And will not God bring about justice for his chosen ones, who cry out to him day and night? Will he keep putting them off? I tell you, he will see that they get justice, and quickly. However, when the Son of Man comes, will he find faith on the earth?" (Luke 18:6-8 KJV)

Jesus encouraged his disciples to be persistent (tether) in prayer. The word *tether* actually means "to tie something with a rope or chain in order to restrict its movement." I like the idea of having my life 'restricted' to the will of God to be bound by His Spirit through prayer. There's no greater freedom. No greater power. When we trust in Jesus, we are bound securely by His faithfulness. God faithfully listens to and answers the prayers of His children. Do you believe this? Even in times when you and I don't feel like He's listening or answering, the Bible assures us that God hears our prayers and responds to each one. And He will complete the good work that He's begun in your life as you seek Him in prayer and tether your heart to His will. I heard someone use this phrase: "You don't throw a whole life away just because it's banged up a little. The reality is that we are all "banged up a little. We all have hidden scars, fresh wounds and broken places. The good news is that God is drawn to broken people. In fact, He accomplishes His greatest work through those who are most broken. Isaiah 45:3 (NIV) "I will give you the treasures of darkness, riches stored in secret places, so that you may know that I am the LORD, the God of Israel, who summons you by name." God has gone before us and in every trial and painful circumstance has buried a treasure or stored rich secrets that can only be found by going through that darkness. The most powerful truths are revealed in the darkest times. In fact, pain intensifies our need for God and can be counted as a blessing.

I remember being in a state of depression. The darkness was an all too familiar companion for most of my life. Over the years, I tried just about everything to soothe the pain - things like success in ministry, the approval of others, perfectionism, doing good things, food and ... you get the idea. In 1995 my carefully constructed world fell apart and I spent two long years at the bottom of a dark pit of depression. I had no idea how to handle the pain and hurt. I cried out to God. He heard my cry and led me to a passage of Scripture that continually heals me and helps me handle the hurt.

Psalm 40:1-3 (NIV) "I waited patiently for the LORD; He turned to me and heard my cry. He lifted me out of the slimy pit, out of the mud and mire; He set my feet on a rock and gave me a firm place to stand. He put a new song in my mouth, a hymn of praise to our God. Many will see and fear and put their trust in the LORD."

I don't know what your particular pit is. But I know what you are feeling. You may be desperately clinging to the broken and mismatched remnants of your life, wondering how you can go on. Whispers of the enemy creep into your heart, soul and mind, taunting you with the lie that you are just too dirty and broken for God to love or use. It seems as if nothing and no one can change that reality, so you might as well give up, just throw in the towel. Stop and pray this prayer!

PRAYER: Lord Please forgive us for all of the times when we have chosen to disconnect. We want to be tethered to Your heart, Lord. We need to be. Help me to set aside my own will and trust in Your plan for my life. Lord help us to admonish the unruly, encourage the fainthearted, help the weak and be patient with everyone. I want to be like trees planted by the streams of water that brings fourth fruit.

I AM

God said to Moses, "I AM WHO I AM. This is what you are to say to the Israelites: 'I am has sent me to you'" (Exodus 3:14 NIV).

In the very first Rocky movie, the Italian Stallion, Rocky Balboa, very eloquently encourages his timid girlfriend, Adriane. "I got gaps. You got gaps. Together we got no gaps." Rocky got it all wrong. He's got gaps. His friend got gaps, and no person alive is going to fill those gaps. God is the only who can fill our gaps. I would go so far as to say that He is the only one who gave us those gaps so that He can fill them. He is the great I AM who fills gaps and fills our blanks.

When we say, "I'm not good enough."

God says, "I AM."

When we say, "I'm not smart enough."

God says, "I AM."

When we say, "I'm not strong enough."

God says, "I AM."

When we say, "I'm not _____ enough."

God says, "I AM."

He is the God who fills in our gaps. He is the God who fills in our blanks.

I've often heard it said there is a God-shaped vacuum in the heart of every man that cannot be filled by another created thing but only by God, the Creator, made known through Jesus Christ. Paul wrote: "[God] said to me . . . for *My* strength *and* power are made perfect (fulfilled and completed) *and show themselves most effective* in [your] weakness" (2 Cor. 12:9, AMPC). Paul knew what he could accomplish on his own: nothing. Oh, he could be busy. We all can do that. But bearing "fruit that remains.

PRAYER: Father God, Your almighty power is balanced with Your tender compassion toward all of creation. It is because of Your abundant mercies that we are not consumed or utterly forsaken. You provide exceedingly more than the bare essentials for our earthly dwelling. Your abiding presence provides faithfulness, stability, and expectant hope for every challenge we face. Thank You for clothing us with dignity, providing us with salvation and for abiding with us day in and day out. Amen.

Reality through Grief

There is a time for everything … a time to weep and a time to laugh, a time to mourn and a time to dance. (Ecclesiastes 3:1,4 KJV)

This month , May 10[t.] 2016 my daughter had her 33rd[th] birthday in heaven. {I'm happy for her. Sad for me.} In a few weeks my first granddaughter who was born two years after Adriane's death, will be graduating from high school and will leave late this summer for a brand new adventure to college. {I'm happy for her. Sad for me.} Goodbyes can give quite a sting, like a sucker punch to the jaw or an upper cut to the gut. My feelings of sorrow are real. Raw!! Strong!! {I wonder if perhaps they are even a bit selfish.} Could be!! For a long time, I used to just take deep breaths and move on. I built invisible walls. Constructed high places emotionally to keep the pain away from my heart. Confident, if not comfortable, that this is what strong Christian women do. We pray, strap on courage, and move forward. Chin up. God's got this. Right?

In the past I'd glance toward sorrow, but would rarely talk to anyone as I processed pain. Not anymore. I've come to realize that sometimes I just need a good cry. God wired us with emotions and I am learning to allow them to be present with me on the road of life instead of pretending they don't exist or really matter.

In the book of Ecclesiastes, Solomon wrote about the gamut of minutes, months, and murk that all of humanity must navigate.

There is a time for everything,
    and a season for every activity under the heavens:

a time to be born and a time to die,
    a time to plant and a time to uproot,
a time to kill and a time to heal,
    a time to tear down and a time to build,

a time to weep and a time to laugh,
    a time to mourn and a time to dance,
a time to scatter stones and a time to gather them,

a time to embrace and a time to refrain from embracing,
a time to search and a time to give up,
  a time to keep and a time to throw away,
a time to tear and a time to mend,
  a time to be silent and a time to speak,
a time to love and a time to hate,
  a time for war and a time for peace.

Ecclesiastes 3:1-8

His Word provides the bounce of perspective I need. It picks me up. Takes my hand and urges me forward. Leads me to His presence. Gives me permission to feel, and to be sad. His grace gives the strength I need to handle the hard emotions. His compassion calmly covers my aches as I go to Him in prayer. The Bible tells us to give thanks in everything. And that God has treasures hidden in dark places that can be found when we search for them. I consider this and choose to thank God in the midst of my grieving. There's a power in praise that doesn't negate sorrow, but does soothe and soften it. As I lift my weary heart to His, I am held by a loving Comforter who catches tears and willingly shares in sadness. And the prayer of my heart becomes…

PRAYER: Lord, Thank you for allowing me to know and love my daughter for 12 years. Thank you for the love we shared as a family. Thank you for the hope I have in Christ that she is in Your presence even now. And thank you for my granddaughter Raegan. Thank you for allowing me to be her "Rammy", (the affectionate name that she gave me for Grandmother). Thank you for the ability You have given her *to* think, reason and dream. Thank You for the amazing plan You have for her life. Help her to walk on the path You are paving for her. You give and take away. I bless your great name, trust Your heart, and give you praise today. In Jesus' name, amen.

Unshakable Peace

I have set the LORD always before me. Because He is at my right
hand, I will not be shaken (Psalm 16:8, NIV).
As you trust Him, God will faithfully fill you with supernatural peace,
strength, and joy. You can experience God's provision through His
Word, through His presence, and through your friends. When your
pantry is empty, God knows. He will send friends to your home with
what you need. When your soul is discouraged, God knows. He sent
reminders of His promises and love through Scripture and through
the encouragement of godly women servants. Despite the fact that
your bank account is bare and the days were still complicated, and
you considered yourself to be wealthier *post-loss* and you know the
soul-level of unshakable peace that is found in Jesus. One thing that
is for sure is the promise of God. As the time of His betrayal and
crucifixion approached, Jesus told his disciples that though they
would grieve His death, their grief would be turned to joy. He
encouraged them to believe all that He said and gave them a
compelling promise.

"I have told you these things, so that in me you may have peace. In
this world you will have trouble. But take heart! I have overcome the
world" (John16:33).

He promised His bewildered disciples that, in Him, they would have
peace in the midst of trouble and how wonderful to know His
promise is valid for us too. No matter what you go through, you can
experience unshakable peace, and declare, "I will not be shaken!" as
the psalmist did in Psalm 16:8. God knows what you have been
through and what you are going through. He promises peace to each
believer through Jesus.

Part of our unsettled nature is that we try to cling to the things of
earth – to the "American way" of living – to the here and now. When
we put our trust in things of this world, we give anxiety, fear,
jealously, discontentment, greed, and insecurity open access to our
lives. (1 Timothy 6:17-19). Instead of finding ways to hold on to what
you have, be encouraged today to let go. Let go of what doesn't
matter. Even let go of those things that seem worth your worry. "So

do not worry, saying, "What shall we eat?" or "What shall we drink?" or "What shall we wear?" For the pagans run after all these things, and your heavenly Father knows that you need them. But seek first his kingdom and his righteousness, and all these things will be given to you as well. Therefore do not worry about tomorrow, for tomorrow will worry about itself. Each day has enough trouble of its own." (Matthew 6:31-34, NIV)

PRAYER: Lord, we feel the peace You have sown into our hearts. We choose to linger there. We drink in your eternal love. Thank You that we are clothed in your forgiveness. We choose always to look to You with all our cares and worries. We release every battle that we know does not belong to us into Your hands. We trust that You can handle it all by yourself. In Jesus, Name

Mother's Day: A Happy & Sad Occasion

One Mother's Day after another passes by since I lost my daughter in October 1995. It does not get easier as years go by. How can this day not intensify my grief after losing one of my two children? Mother's Day will never be the same ever! This day that used to bring me joy will always be blended with sadness. It is yet another reminder that one of my children left a big void in my home and life.

On this day, I always have the wish to go back in time to when both children woke up early on this special day to see their smiling faces, the cards they drew and presents they thoughtfully bought. Unfortunately, such a wish does not come true, but I carry this beautiful memory in my heart all day long every Mother's Day.

The last time I had a complete Mother's Day was in 1994 when both my children were still at home. Later that year, my oldest moved out. I celebrated the last Mother's Day with my youngest, my deceased daughter, in May 1995. The following year, I spent the morning of Mother's day alone. I always felt something was missing when one of my children was away on Mother's Day and other special occasions, but it never occurred to me that I would have a day as a bereaved mother. My sadness does not need a trigger on this day as it never leaves me but there are things that happen that heighten my feelings more overtly. I received a Mother's Day message from a friend that implied that mothers outlive their children. My tears flooded my face. Mother's Day is hard enough for bereaved mothers; but people tend to forget this. I do hope that mothers do not take for granted their children being alive as much as the children celebrate their mothers.

Every moment should be treasured between a mother and her child on this special day and throughout the year, as we can never guarantee that we can have another Mother's Day together. All this does not make me forget my blessings. I am very fortunate to have my son and grandbabies and a wonderful husband who are thoughtful and in their special way try to make Mother's Day easier on me. They are the ones who fill the void of me not having my baby girl here with me on Mother's Day, a day that she was born on.

PRAYER: "Lord, there is not a single minute of my life when this loss is not etched so keenly into my brain and heart, whether it is in the middle of a busy day or in those choking moments of grief in the solitary dark of night. Let me be grateful for every minute we had together. Let me treasure those memories and find joy in them. Help me to deal with people better. They don't know what to say. They stumble and look away when they see me. They pretend nothing has happened. I know they "don't want to remind me" but they don't understand it is with me always, always.

"Teach me, Lord. Tell me what you want me to do with this. What am I supposed to learn from this kind of pain? What are you calling me to do? "Open my battered heart and lead me to comfort and peace. Only you can give me the peace I need. Let me feel your presence in my life."

Myths about Grief

MYTH: The pain will go away faster if you ignore it.

Fact: Trying to ignore your pain or keep it from surfacing will only make it worse in the long run. For real healing it is necessary to face your grief and actively deal with it. Lean into it go with it.

MYTH: It's important to be "be strong" in the face of loss.

Fact: Feeling sad, frightened, or lonely is a normal reaction to loss. Crying doesn't mean you are weak. You don't need to "protect" your family or friends by putting on a brave front. Showing your true feelings can help them and you.

MYTH: If you don't cry, it means you aren't sorry about the loss.

Fact: Crying is a normal response to sadness, but it's not the only one. Those who don't cry may feel the pain just as deeply as others. They may simply have other ways of showing it.

MYTH: Grief should last about a year.

Fact: There is no right or wrong time frame for grieving. How long it takes can differ from person to person.

PRAYER: Lord, I am crying out to you. My emotions are screaming at me. Lord I feel alone. Sadness surrounds me, and depression is pulling me down. I long for what I have lost. I ache. My loss permeates my mind and emotions. My grief tries to influence the course of most of my waking moments. Father, help me process this loss. Help me move forward. Help me to welcome joy into those place. Help me turn my mourning into joy. Lord, I need to draw nearer to you. You are the hope of my salvation through this dark place. In Jesus Mighty Name, Amen

Winning over Worry

Always give thanks to God the Father for everything in the name of our Lord Jesus Christ (Ephesians 5:20, NCV).

One of my friends that lives in South Florida, mentioned to me how the grass in their yards grew year round. So did the weeds. I learned in our conversation that the best way to deal with weeds was simply to take really good care of the grass. When the grass was healthy, it was thick and lush – leaving little room for weeds to grow.

When our hearts and lives are filled with praise, worry is a weed that will die from lack of attention. When we choose to continually give God thanks, there will be little room in our hearts for fear.

Why?

Because praise acknowledges the very character of God, while thanksgiving recognizes the work of His hand. Together, praise and thanksgiving are powerful weapons against worry and formidable tools to strengthen our faith. I know what you are thinking. Sometimes it is just plain hard to praise God because of the grueling circumstances we are facing. Honestly, it is hard to find something to celebrate.

The problem is that we don't understand the true meaning of praise. Praise comes from a Latin word that means "value" or "worth." To praise God means to celebrate His worth, His value and His presence. "Sing to God, sing praise to His name, extol Him who rides on the clouds—His name is the Lord—and rejoice before Him" (Psalm 68:4).

Praise and thanksgiving pleases God. Psalm 147:1 "How good it is to sing praise to our God, how pleasant and fitting to praise Him!"

Praise and thanksgiving encourage obedience. 1 Thessalonians 5:16-18 "Be joyful always; pray continually; give thanks in all circumstances, for this is God's will for you in Christ Jesus." Did you catch the truth that it is His *will* for us to praise Him? Obedience to Him always promotes peace and eliminates worry.

Praise and thanksgiving enhance our awareness of His presence. Psalm 22:3 (NIV) "But You are holy, enthroned in the praises of Israel." When we praise God, we enthrone Him in our lives. We make that fearful circumstance His dwelling place. That's right! We invite Jesus to join us in our mess. Do you know that He always accepts that invitation of praise? Praise and thanksgiving produce trust. Psalm 42:11 Easy Read Version (ERV) asks, "Why am I so sad? Why am I so upset? I should put my hope in God and keep praising Him. The psalmist is telling his own soul to stop the pity party, put his hope in God and keep praising Him – no matter what!

Thanksgiving is a deposit on the future. Praise is trusting Him for what He will do and then expecting Him to do it, understanding that today's stumbling blocks are tomorrow's stepping-stones. Praise frees God to work because when we praise Him, we are choosing to trust Him, despite the circumstances.

I heard this story told of a young man who was sitting on a park bench reading his Bible. Suddenly he began to shout. "Praise the Lord! What a miracle!" Maybe, this story will encourage you. An older, very distinguished man walking by stopped and asked what he was so excited about. The young man replied, "I was just reading how God parted the Red Sea and the whole nation of Israel walked across on dry ground." The older man sneered, "You know"? That wasn't a real sea at all. It was just a few inches of water." He then turned in irritation and walked away, leaving the young man confused and discouraged. But in a few minutes the young man began to shout again. The unbeliever returned asking, "What are you shouting about now?" "I just read how God drowned the whole Egyptian army in just a few inches of water!" Hilarious!!!

Don't let anyone keep you from praising God.

PRAYER: Lord I adore and praise you for being that protection that I need in time of trouble. Thank you for the angels that encamp about me. So here I am in the place of worship, eyes open, drinking in your strength and glory. In your generous love I am really living at last. My lips sing praises like fountains. I bless you every time I talk a breath. My arms wave like a crazy woman praises to you. I love you Lord with my whole heart. Lord you are worthy and I honor you. Amen

Peace that surpasses ALL understanding:

Ten years after my daughter Adriane's life was taken, God came back and got my Daddy, who was one of my best friends after not having a relationship for a few years because of me not being happy because he was not in the home where I was raised by my mother. After writing a letter and forgiving him, my sisters and I prepared dinner, being obedient to the voice of God, washed his feet and shared our hearts. Our relationship became stronger.

He was diagnosed with lung cancer a few years after this experience. Talking about God using this for good!! After hearing the news about the cancer, my family got together every Tuesday night to speak life into him, had praise and worship and prayer. Even the little ones that age ranged from 8-16. God moved so miraculously through the babies that Dad was encouraged that if God was ready for him, he was ready to go. One year later Dad went on to be with the Lord. He stated to us that he just wanted to see his grandson (my son) get married. On the way back from the wedding he stated, "All is well". "I got to see my grandson get married"! It was as if he and God made a bargain like Hezekiah, when he asked God to give him 10 more years to live.

All Dad wanted was a few months. He transitioned on October 22, 2005 leaving us with, "Everybody wants to go to heaven, but nobody wants to die. He turned he face to the wall, started singing, laughing and speaking in tongues. What a way to leave this earth!!

PRAYER: Lord thank you for giving me the key to living in peace. So many live without it, and I can have it. Help me order my thoughts and direct my mind to think on the things rather than being influenced or driven by what I see, hear and feel. As I do so, I will have YOUR peace in life every day.

LORD, there are times when the struggle of life seems longer than I can endure, the weariness more than I can, and the cost of survival more than I can pay. In those times, help me not forget the joy You have prepared for me in the end--as well as the promises of strength and power to overcome that I have through You now. In Jesus' name, Amen. Revelations 21:3-4.

Like few other emotions, anger restricts and binds us, tying us in eternal knots. Forgiveness, on the other hand, sets us free from those bonds, untying the knots that hold us captive. The Lord Jesus said, "Forgive, and you will be forgiven" (Luke 6:37).

When Life Seems Broken

In Nehemiah 1:13 (New International Version), the bible shows us that Nehemiah prayed. He was pressed but not crushed. He told the Lord that he was sorry for the way he and his people had rejected God and for the ways they had disobeyed His commands. He remembered the instructions of God to His people and reminded Him of His promises. And he asked God to hear his prayer, give him favor and lead his responses. Are there complications that have your heart grieving and sifting through ashes? Perhaps you are trying to keep a stiff upper lip and carry those broken burdens quietly? Know today that God is all about rebuilding broken hearts and hopes. He specializes in transforming smoky ash heaps into beautiful displays of His grace. He moves you toward that beauty and healing as you move toward Him in distress as Nehemiah did. Stuff just happens!! Life just happens. There are all kinds of things going on that you can do absolutely nothing about at all. They are totally outside your control. Of course, there are other things over which we have some control, but let's face it. Probably all of us could testify right now to circumstances that some days affects our lives and just *happens*. Anyway, the Bible tells us that while there is no question that life happens, we are responsible to live wisely and well while our life is happening.

Now, the question is, Where do we find out what to do while our life is happening? The answer to that, of course, is from the Word of God. We find in *John 14:27*, Peace I leave with you; My peace I give to you; not as the world gives do I give to you. Do not let your heart be troubled, nor let it be fearful. (NASB). *Romans 8:28*

And we know that God causes everything to work together for the good of those who love God and are called according to his purpose for them. (NLT). God reminds us that He is always there to support and guide us when bad things happen. Tough times mean being tough ourselves, and God is there to carry us through. He provides us with what we need.

PRAYER: Lord your words says that you will perfect everything that concerns us even when you are silent. Lord, I thank you for finishing what you started in me. Because I know You are with me, I can be strong and courageous in the face of challenging situations. I can be confident of what You will do because I know Your ways and Your character through Your Word and promises to me. Help me understand Your word and make the study of it a greater priority in my life every day. Help me learn to rely upon it and appreciate its wisdom in my life. In Jesus' name, Amen.

We Can't Live Without Hope

People can live for forty days without food, four days without water, and four minutes without air. But we cannot live for four seconds without hope. When faced with a temptation to be dishonest, to steal, to lie, or to lust, look to the emotional reservoir of hope for the strength to hold fast to the way of righteousness, and deny yourself some brief, unsatisfying pleasure. It can work for you. This is the way to fight for holiness in the Christian life. This is the biblical way to make our calling and election sure. My prayer is that as we focus our attention on Christian hope, God will fill your reservoir to overflowing, and that deep down in the debts of our soul will generate joy and love, boldness and endurance will stir up new power for the glory of God. Are you going to continue this craziness? For only crazy people would think they could be complete by their own efforts what was begun by God. If you weren't smart enough to begin it, how do you suppose you could perfect it? Did you go through this whole painful learning process for nothing? It is not yet a total loss, but it certainly will be if you keep this up? Answer this question. Does God who lavishly provides for you with His own presence, His Holy Spirit, working things in your lives, you could never do for yourselves, unconditional love towards us. No matter what we face in life, we can trust that God is in control. We must rely on Him and His goodness. Does he do things because of your strenuous moral striving or because you trust Him to do them in you. Gal. 3:3-5 Message Bible. Great suffering well borne, is an indication of unshakable faith in God. Faith in God must be maintained through times of trial as well as through times of blessings. Such faith reflects God' nature in us. His redeeming power in Christ, and the His glory.

PRAYER: Lord, I value even the painful things I have experienced because I have learned from them totally and they have given me a greater understanding of you. I am closer to you today because of them. To lose what I gained from these experiences would be a great loss. Never let it be so. Help me to always trust you and know that you will continue to work for good in my life as I trust you to do so. In Jesus Name.

Why me Lord!!!!

How often have you cried out to God, Why? Why is justice perverted? Why don't people understand me? Why do the unjust prosper? The answer: Because you are anointed!! I used to have the wrong notion that when you are really anointed, you no longer have problems or rough times. Show me anybody who's really Holy Ghost filled, tongue-talking, casting-out-demons, anointed, and I'll show you somebody who cried in the middle of the night, wondering where is God. (Me) I have to confess that through it all I have learned to trust in Jesus. Through it all, I've learned to trust in God.

I remember thinking when I would hear about someone going through with the loss (a word that I don't like to use, especially when you know where they are) of a loved one through sudden or violent death, "I feel so sorry for them." "I don't know what I would do if that were me. Anointed does not have anything to do with going through. It can help with who you're going through it with. I don't understand how people go through life not knowing God.

There is something else that happens on earth that does not seem fair. Bad things should happen to bad people and good things should happen to good people. But, sometimes bad things happen to good people and good things happen to bad people. That is not fair!!! Eccles. 8:14

I have strength for all things in Christ Who empowers me [I am ready for anything and equal to anything through Him Who infuses inner strength into me; I am self-sufficient in Christ's sufficiency].

Philippians 4:13 (Read all of Philippians 4:13)

Amplified Bible
Prayer: Lord, when I see unfair things or they happen to me, help me trust that you are working for my good, even if it doesn't look or feel like it. There is so much that I don't understand, but can understand that you love me.

Praise

Psalm 145 gives us 22 reasons to praise God – all based on *who* God is and *what* he does for us. That's almost as many reasons as verses in the chapter! He is a personal God, he is sovereign King. God is great, unsearchable and God acts on our behalf. God is majestic, good, righteous, gracious and full of compassion. God is slow to anger, merciful, powerful, makes himself known to us. God helps us, provides for us and is generous. God is near to us, listens, saves, preserves us and brings justice. There is power in His presence and in our praise. There will be times when you don't feel like worshipping. But when you get a revelation that's about Him and not you, you will learn to worship Him even when you don't feel like it! You know you are growing in the Lord if you can praise the Lord, despite how you feel or what it looks like.

I remember getting dressed for my baby girl's home going service. I heard a song playing mentioning praise him in advance. My thought was praise for what. I'm hurting!! A scripture came to mind in I Peter 4:12-13, Beloved, think it not strange concerning the fiery trial which is to try you, as though some strange thing happened unto you: 13 But rejoice, inasmuch as ye are partakers of Christ's sufferings; that, when his glory shall be revealed, ye may be glad also with exceeding joy. In service one night I heard a preacher paraphrase this scripture by saying, "In verse 13, "But rejoice", he stated, "to have a party". I looked up and said, "God if there is going to be a party you probably should start it". Shortly after that I has a praise in my feet. Tears flowing.
I do know that this was not coming from my flesh but by the Holy Spirit. Set your heart on the truth of who God is as revealed in Christ. If worship is fire, then truth is the fuel that causes the fire to burn. The more fuel, the hotter the fire. So focus prayerfully and relentlessly on the truth in the songs, the prayers, the Scriptures so that you can praise Him with no limits or worries.

I will praise you, Oh Lord, among the nations. I will sing of you among the people. For great is your love, reaching to the heavens, your faithfulness reaches to the skies. Be exalted Oh God above the heavens; Let your glory be over all the earth. Ps. 57:9:11

PRAYER: Lord thank you for being the One I can always trust, and for being the One who has never failed me, even in times that I failed you. People are sometimes unfaithful, but you are always faithful in all that you have promised. They can have selfish motives or unreasonable expectations, but Your love is unconditional. I just need to say, "Be exalted, O God!! Amen

Total Forgiveness

Total forgiveness is when you can talk about a situation and not feel what you felt in the initial account. It also means that when you come in contact with the person or persons you can be cordial with them. I remember having the chance to visit the facility where the young men were that took my daughter's life. My heart was so heavy for them when expectantly, I saw one of them come down the hall that we were touring. I felt a need to pray because I could feel the evil and dark side of that place that could make you being there react to the atmosphere. Spirits don't care who they attach themselves to. Forgiveness came one day after the shooting because of a seed that was planted through a preached word from my pastor about the subject.

On October 17th that seed took root and it all came from my spirit and not from my flesh, the emotional side of me. This story in Matthew resonated when the words, "I forgive came from my lips. My thought was one day I will need forgiveness from God. If I can't forgive, I will miss the opportunity when the time comes for me to ask. Forgiveness is another way of admitting, I am human, I make mistakes. I want to be granted privilege and so I grant you that privilege. You have to keep on doing it.

The King summoned the man and said, "You evil servant"!! I forgave your entire debt when you begged me for mercy. Shouldn't you be compelled to be merciful to your fellow servant who asked you for mercy? The King was furious and put the screws to the man until he paid back the entire debt. And that's exactly what my Father in heaven is going to do to each one of you who doesn't forgive unconditionally anyone who ask for mercy. Matthew 18:32-35 Forgiveness warms the heart and cools the sting.

Matthew 6:12 "And forgive us our debts, as we forgive our debtors". When was the last time you really wanted God to forgive your sins the same way you forgive people who hurt you?
Habakkuk 2:3 ESV For still the vision awaits its appointed time; it hastens to the end—it will not lie. If it seems slow, wait for it; it will surely come; it will not delay.

PRAYER: Lord, you forgave all my sins and made a debt free to you. But when someone intentionally does me wrong, it feels like a different matter. I want to hold them responsible for what they have done. Help me see it as one and the same. As you freely forgive me and cancelled my debt to you. Help me to extend that same mercy, and forgiveness and release to those who hurt me to you. Amen

He May Not Come When You Want Him, But He Is Always On Time

Often we wonder why God does not seem to be answering our prayers. But I learned growing up in the Baptist church from some older members in African-American churches that I was a part of: "God may not come when you want him to, but he's always right on time." Those wise older believers who had been through so much yet had seen God's faithfulness were right about how God works in the long run. "God may not come when you want him to, but he's always right on time." I do believe that timing is everything.

There are some things I've been waiting on God to do in my life a long time, but I'm not discouraged that time has elapsed and I'm growing older… What to do when you have been seeking God for a long time and it has not come to pass? This is what I recommend. I recommend that you keep your request before God if you know God said this is the plan for your life. I found in waiting that you must have FAITH. Don't ever give up on your dreams.

What God promised to you will come to pass because He is an on time God that may not come when we want him, but he will be there right on time, so just hold on to God's unchanging hand… He will never leave you or forsake you…. He will never put you down, and make you feel less than a person while you wait. Just trust in him and keep the faith and know that all things work for the good according to God's purpose and God's plan.

PRAYER: Lord, for a long time I wondered if you heard my prayers. But, then, you answered. I saw that your delay was for my good. You have shown me that I could trust you even when I doubt you and do not feel your presence or protection. Thank you for the assurance that you will always hear me and do what is best. Help me lift my voice and my heart to you in gratitude and acknowledgement of all you have done for me. I praise you Lord, for answering my prayer. You are my strong shield and I trust you completely. You have helped me, and I will celebrate and thank you in song. Ps. 28:6-7 KJV

Being vulnerable and making sudden decisions while grieving
Story

After a death of a loved one we are vulnerable and are quick to make decisions without thinking. If you're contemplating something that would affect your finances, you can likewise discuss it with a trusted friend or confidant but you should also seek the opinion of a professional financial advisor. Having a conversation with someone who has your best interest at heart can help you gain a better sense of perspective and, perhaps, help you realize that the situation is less urgent than it feels to you.

About a month after Adriane's death, someone mentioned getting rid of her things. That was the hardest thing for me to do. When I did decide, I did not want to do this alone. I called all her close friends to help and allowed them to take what they wanted as a memory of her. Doing it this way made it so easy for me to let go of her things. Of course I kept some things for myself like her cheerleaders uniform, a dress that she wore in my sisters' wedding and all her sculptures angels and Christmas ornaments.

The most important thing you can do is to take care of yourself while you're grieving. Grief is hard work and takes a genuine physical, mental, emotional and spiritual toll on our bodies, minds, and hearts. Unfortunately, the old adage that "time heals all wounds" isn't true following the death of someone close. Instead, we *gradually* assimilate the loss of a loved one into our new lives and learn to live with the scar on our heart, but we never truly forget the person who died. For now, trust that you will eventually reach that state, and try to avoid making any major life decisions in haste while your grief feels freshest.

PRAYER: Lord, what the enemy says sometimes sounds so close to what you say!! We can get so caught up in our own excitement or desires that we fail to recognize who is speaking. Give me greater discernment to distinguish the difference between your voices, his voice ad my own voice. Help me to not be misled by the enemy or my own thoughts and feelings.

Worship while in the Valley

All of us go through valley experiences in life. Adversity is an inevitable part of life. When difficulties come, we tend to wonder why God has allowed us to suffer. We may even feel abandoned by Him. But Scripture tells us otherwise.

Psalm 23 describes the Lord caring for us as tenderly and faithfully as a shepherd cares for his flock. This beloved passage of God's Word is a reminder that He is always present—loving, protecting, and guiding us. He has a purpose for every adversity He allows.

When life seems unbearable, you and I have to make a commitment to vent up, when we consistently take our concerns (and complaints) to God, something unique happens. Tragedy and worship are inseparable!!! At our lowest moments, God is still ever present. He is ever faithful. To know Him is to worship Him. I can remember being in this valley experience, all I wanted to do was read my word and stay in worship. I have learned that this is where the Lord speaks and give directions. I was reminded of when the Lord prepared me for what I was about to go through before the death of my baby girl. He showed me a dream, a song that was always playing on the radio every time I got in and out of my car, and a conversation my daughter and.

Don't despise the valley experience. They prepare you for the journey, unharmed, for how you go through and come out as pure gold. There was a young lady on my job that thought that I was walking around with my head up thinking that I was better than anyone. But what she failed to realize was that my looking up was looking for God to help me through my journey of grief. I knew all my answers were UP.

As I explained this to her, she apologized numerous times because she had not been in this position before. A few years later, she had to bury her daughter who had been sick for a long time. She called me to apologize again because she could now understand where I was. Some people think that having loved ones leave this earth the grieving is the same. I beg the differ!! The first person in my family to die was my grandmother. She was my best friend who I could talk to about anything. Years later, my baby brother drowned while taking swimming lessons, the feeling of not having him around, I felt a certain way. Next was my baby girl, a pain that hurt to the pit of my stomach. There was this empty feeling, an empty hole, that I felt and still feel to this day. My father past 10 years after her and again I felt different with this one. My father and I were very close, but when he shared with me that he had made his peace with the Lord and if he was ready for him, he was ready to go home. Cancer was the culprit to his death.

No one can completely escape all suffering in life. But as believers, we can face difficulties with confidence. If you are in a valley right now, I pray that you will remember God as your faithful Shepherd. He will guide you through heartache and show you how to overcome in His strength. Look to Him for peace and hope despite your circumstances. If you are willing to walk with Him through the valley, you will experience God's highest blessing on the next mountaintop.

Here are a few things that I learned while in the valley. I have added some things that will help you while you are in the valley: Practice what you learned while in the Valley (Peace)There is a correct way to respond to valleys.
A. Surrender your life to God.

B. Believe that the Lord will use this experience for good (Rom. 8:28).

C. Rest in His wisdom, love, and power.

D. Thank Him for bringing you through the valley. You will learn invaluable lessons in life's darkest seasons.

PRAYER: Thank You Father that You are the faithful, good and righteous God. You are the Lord who always keeps Your promises. You are the God who is gracious and merciful in salvation, even as You are just and wrathful in Your judgments. We thank You for Your faithfulness throughout the centuries, throughout the millennia; You have always kept Your promises, Your plans for our salvation have been unwavering. In Jesus Name

Forgiving Others and Ourselves

We need to understand three things about forgiveness. First, we can never be good enough or do enough to buy it. Second, forgiveness is not for sale, nor can we earn it. Third, if we have a personal relationship with Jesus Christ, then all the forgiveness we will ever need already belongs to us. But we must choose to experience that forgiveness by accepting it as a free gift of God.

Our pride is often the biggest obstacle to experiencing forgiveness.

Our pride is often the biggest obstacle to forgiving others.

True forgiveness always requires sacrifice on our part – a truth that may often seem unfair in human terms. After all, we are the ones who have been hurt. Why should we have to sacrifice anything? Shouldn't the people who hurt us be the ones who have to make the first move and offer the biggest sacrifice?

True forgiveness – God's forgiveness – defies human logic and cannot be explained in human terms. Human forgiveness is easier … but a shallow substitute and a cheap imitation for the amazing power of God's forgiveness.

We need to be willing to take the first step in the process of forgiveness. Jesus was. Romans 5:8 tells us that "God shows His great love for us in this way: Christ died for us while we were still sinners."

Jesus died for people who do not deserve forgiveness, people who refuse to ask for forgiveness, people who ignore their own faults, people who sit in judgment of others, people who insist on others taking the first step. People like you and me.

We need to love and forgive in the same way.
Jesus has forgiven every sin----not only the wrong things you have done, but every wrong thing you ever will do. He has already paid for your sins and errors by shedding His blood on the cross for them and determined to cleanse you from them.

I John 1:7
"The Blood of Jesus Christ, God's son cleanses (removes) us from ALL sin and guilt. (Keeps us cleansed from sin in all forms and manifestations.

When our strength is in God, even the difficult places in life can be turned into blessings. That's why we need to constantly keep our minds and hearts focused on Him: not our circumstances.
PS. 84:5-7 Happy are those who are strong in the Lord, who want above all else to follow your direction for their lives. When you walk in the valley of weeping, it will become a place of springs where pools of blessings and refreshment collect after rains. You will grow constantly in strength, and each of them invited to meet the Lord in Zion.

"If I'm worried or upset, my focus isn't on God, and I have not left it in his hands.

Prayer: I am forgiven from all sins. I do not have to feel guilt or shame again. Lord, thank you for your forgiveness.

<u>Release</u>

I met a mother in Chattanooga whose son's life was taken hanging out with his friends shooting dice. He won and one of the other young men didn't think he won fair so he shot and killed him. After burying him and dealing with other matter concerning him, Mom never released him to the Lord.

Everyone goes through grieving differently and uniquely. She felt having a party at the cemetery and continuing to fix his plate for dinner every night would make her feel better about him being gone. I was able to give her insight on releasing him to the Lord so that she could focus more on her other children that needed her.
Release- To relieve from something that confines, burdens, or oppresses. To stop holding, (something or someone. Greek word meaning Catharsis: the purging of emotions.

Once she understood what I was sharing with her she stated that as she released him, she felt a weight lift off of her that she could not understand. Trusting God without question is faith. Our strength comes from letting go and letting God do what only He can. Sometimes we have to lose something or someone in order to gain. We hold on to things or people and cannot see past them until they are removed. Many times, they have served their purpose in us but we yet want to hold on.

PRAYER: Lord, I place all my worries, fears, circumstances and anything or anyone that causes me to lose my focus on you. Matthew 5:4 Blessed are they who mourn, for they shall be comforted. Whatever you let go of, will be replaced. You are blessed when you mourn losses because it's when the power of God can come and show us His comforting power!! Blessed are you, when you feel you've lost what is most dear to you, because that's when Jesus can become most dear to you.

The feeling of being not worthy

God will take the truth and massage it into your broken heart like a
healing ointment. He will place a crown of beauty on your head and
wash away the ashes. He will give you the oil of gladness instead of
mourning, and dress you in a garment of praise instead of despair.
No longer will your identity be determined by what happened to you
in your past. Our identity is determined by what happens in us
through Jesus Christ." In you Lord I have taken refuge: let me never
be put to shame, deliver me in your righteousness. Turn your ear to
me, come quickly to my rescue, be my rock of refuge, a strong
fortress to save me. For the sake of your name lead and guide me,
free me from the trap that is set for me. For you are my refuge. Ps.
31:1-4
It's not unusual to feel sad from time to time. Sometimes we feel
down because of something that we experience – a disappointment, a
break-up, a disagreement with a friend, or a really tragic movie.
Sometimes we feel sad and don't even know why. There are things
we can all do to reduce the feelings of sadness in our lives like having
a good support network, focusing on positive thoughts or taking care
of ourselves.

When you feel depressed, check your thinking. It is not God's will for
us to be depressed or despondent. Summing it all up, friends, I'd say
you will have to do your best by filling your minds and meditating on
the things true, noble, reputable, authentic, compelling, gracious, the
best, not the worst, the beautiful, not the ugly, the things to praise,
not the things to curse.

Phil. 4:8 "If you are depressed, dig deeper into the word of God. It
is there where you will find joy. Christ's peace acts like a spiritual
radar. It helps make our powers of discernment more effective.
Prayer: Lord please remind me when I am depressed that I need to
meditate on your word.

Prayer: Lord , thank you for being my refuge, my rock, my safe place. Regardless of what happens in my life I can survive because I trust you will make a way for me. Thank you for being my rock, my safe place,

I come to You with a heart humbled by Your tender love for me. I thank You that You have removed the filthy rags of this world from my life and clothed me with the righteousness of Christ. Help me to hold my head high as a child of the King. In Jesus' Name

New Garment

The Lord will provide for those that grieve…a garment of praise instead of a spirit of despair. They will be called oaks of righteousness, a planting of the Lord for the display of His splendor. Is. 61:3 NIV

Do you need a garment today? I'm talking about a physical garment. I'm talking about what's covering you mind and emotions. Are you clothed with despair and disappointment? Is your garment heavy? If you have gone through a time of separation or a hurtful situation, the Bible says there is a time to grieve, and is important to release that hurt to the Lord. The Bible also tells us that God wants to give you a garment of praise instead of a spirit of despair. Are your garments of yesterday weighing you down and holding you back? The garment of praise is light and filled with peace and joy. Today is the day for a new garment. Forgive, release and praise Him for restoration, even if you don't feel or see it. Display the glory of the Lord all the days of your life.

PRAYER: Father, I come to you today asking that you take off my old garments of despair and heaviness. Make me new in Christ today. Give me a garment of praise to show your glory in the earth in the mist of adversity.

<u>Love vs Evil:</u>

Make sure that no one pays back wrong for wrong, but always pray, be kind to one another. Be joyful always, pray continually; give thanks in all circumstances. For this is the will of the Lord for you in Christ Jesus. I Thess. 5:15-18

There are two main reasons why Christians should not chose evil over love. One is that *it reveals something of the way God is.* God is merciful. "He makes his sun rise on the evil and on the good, and sends rain on the just and on the unjust" (Matthew 5:45). "He does not deal with us according to our sins, nor repay us according to our iniquities" (Psalm 103:10). "Be kind to one another, tenderhearted, forgiving one another, as God in Christ forgave you" (Ephesians 4:32). So when Christians live this way, we show something of what God is like.

I've seen through most deaths that I have encountered, there is some kind of division or fight that comes about, whether it pertains to money, who pays for what or Just plain ole, they were closer to me than you or I did this or that for them. I believe that is the hand of the enemy to try and keep God from getting the glory. This makes us go through the grief with no hope.

The second reason is that *the hearts of Christians are satisfied with God and are not driven by the craving for revenge or self-exaltation or money or earthly security.* God has become our all-satisfying treasure and so we don't treat our adversaries out of our own sense of need and insecurity, but out of our own fullness with the satisfying glory of God. What takes away the compulsion of revenge is our deep confidence that this world is not our home, and that God is our utterly sure and all-satisfying reward.

So in both these reasons for loving our enemy we see the main thing: God is shown to be who he really is as a merciful God and as gloriously all-satisfying. The ultimate reason for being merciful is to glorify God—to make him look great in the eyes of man.

I speak, to many of you who are trying to keep your head above water, but you feel like you are going down for the third time. The waves created by the storms of life have overwhelmed you. But, I say to you, do not be despaired: do not give up hope. God is your present help in time of trouble and will bring you through these times of adversity in triumph. Trust Him, and let him guide your steps to make your way perfect.

Refuse to allow the enemy to make you feel like you have to fight every battle, for God is with you. He sees what you are having to face and endure, Keep your faith in me says the Lord, and persevere. James 5:11 Indeed we count them blessed who endure. You have heard of perseverance of Job and seen the end intended by the Lord. The Lord is very compassionate and merciful.

PRAYER: Lord, thank you for teaching me that I can live without being compelled to respond in vengeance when someone does wrong to me. Help me respond in a Jesus way to pray and love them, which will cause greater change in their lives than my anger cold accomplish. Continue to change me and help me to grow in you, even if others do not change.

Totally Forgive:

Total forgiveness is when you can talk about a situation that not feel what you felt in the initial account and when you come in contact with the person or person you can be cordial with them. I remember having the chance to visit the facility where the young men were that took my daughter's life. My heart was so heavy for them when expectantly, I saw one of them come down the hall that we were touring. I felt a need to pray because I could feel the evil and dark side of that place that could make you being there react to the atmosphere. Spirits don't care who it attach itself to.

Forgiveness came one day after the shooting because of a seed that was planted through a preached word from my pastor about the subject. On October 17th that seed took root and it all came from my spirit and not from my flesh, the emotional side of me. This story in Matthew resonated when the words, "I forgive came from my lips. My thought was one day I will need forgiveness from God. If I can't forgive, I will miss the opportunity when the time comes for me to ask. The King summoned the man and said, "You evil servant"!! I forgave your entire debt when you begged me for mercy. Shouldn't you be compelled to be merciful to your fellow servant who asked you for mercy? The King was furious and put the screws to the man until he paid back the entire debt. And that's exactly what my Father in heaven is going to do to each one of you who doesn't forgive unconditionally anyone who ask for mercy. Matthew 18:32-35

PRAYER: Lord, you forgave all my sins and made a debt free to you. But when someone intentionally does me wrong, it feels like a different matter. I want to hold them responsible for what they have done. Help me see it as one and the same. As you freely forgive me and cancelled my debt to you. Help me to extend that same mercy, and forgiveness and release to those who hurt me to you. Amen me. In Jesus Name, Amen

How to Find Your Missing Peace

I'm sure you have heard about the Good News for the people of Israel - that there is peace with God through Jesus Christ, who is Lord of all (Acts 10:36, NLT).

I heard a story of a little girl who was working very hard on her homework one night. As the hours went by, her parents became very curious and asked her what she was doing. "I'm writing a report on the condition of the world and how to bring peace," she replied. Her parents were impressed! "Isn't that a big assignment for just one person?" her dad asked. With complete confidence the little girl responded, "Don't worry, Dad. There are three of us in the class working on it." Wouldn't it be wonderful if finding and experiencing peace was that easy?

We work hard at peace - in our world, in our homes, in our relationships, and in our hearts. Yet, so many of us struggle to actually experience or even understand true peace. It occurs to me that in order to understand what peace *is,* we must first understand what it *is not.*

True peace is God's peace and can only be found in Him. God's peace is not the absence of conflicts, trials or difficulties and has nothing to do with human beings or human circumstances. In fact, the true peace of God cannot be produced on a human level at all. Any peace that can be explained by human logic is very fragile and will surely be destroyed by the storms of life.

I don't know about you, but storms seem to sweep through my life on a regular basis and peace is often nowhere to be found. If we rely on this spoiled and fallen world for any measure of peace, we will forever be disappointed.

The only source of peace is God.

The only way to know peace is to know God.

The apostle Paul said, "There is peace with God through Jesus Christ, who is Lord of all."

We tend to focus on the part of that verse that promises peace with God and ignore the harder truth that peace is the result of Jesus reigning in our lives as "Lord of all." The word "Lord" means "boss" and drives home the point that if Jesus is not Lord *of* all – He is not Lord *at* all.

And if He is not the Lord of all, then there can be no peace.

I'm sure you have read the poem below. Even though I often run across it on Facebook, or someone emails it to me, I never read it without being encouraged to remember exactly where my peace is found.

"I'm too blessed to be stressed and too anointed to be disappointed.
I refuse to be discouraged, to be sad or to cry.
I refuse to be downhearted and here's the reason why:
I have a God who is almighty; who is sovereign and supreme.
I have a God who loves me – and I am on His team.
He is all wise and powerful; Jesus is His name.
Though everything else is changeable, My God remains the same.
I refuse to be beaten or defeated.
My eyes are on my God.
He has promised to be with me, as through this life I trod.
I am looking past my circumstances, to heaven's throne above.
My prayers have reached the heart of God, and I am resting in His love.
I give thanks to Him in everything". Unknown

PRAYER: Father, Son and the Holy Spirit, our guide and inspiration, lead us to the right direction. And if, on our way, we encounter difficulties and trials, do not allow us to fall or lose hope. Grant us the graces we need every day that we may also share our blessings with your people. And when the time comes, Holy Spirit, lead us to the place that is safe, full of joy and eternal peace. Amen

On the next pages you can journal your feelings to bring
healing and restoration during your grieving process.

In Loving Memory of my precious daughter Adriane Nicole Dickerson 5/10/1983-10/17/1995

Adriane Nicole was the little girl that I asked God for. At 12 years old

He asked for her back. Although I was devastated to let her go I

know without a doubt that she is safe. Never getting to see her as a

teenage and getting to experience all that teenagers go through.

proms and dates and hanging out with her girlfriends, learning to

drive and taking those shopping trips that we often took. Her quite

but quirky spirit and great sense of humor. She is now a beautiful

rose in God's garden.

Made in the USA
Monee, IL
20 September 2019